Suhana Rossi

Harz
Travel Guide

Title: Harz Travel Guide
Author: Suhana Rossi
Published by: NEXTUNICORN PUBLISHER PROPRIETORSHIP
Publisher's Address: Shree Dwarkadhish Ji Ka Was, Emri, Rajsamand, RAJASTHAN, India. Pincode: 313342
Printer Details: Published online on various platforms.
Edition: 01
ISBN: 978-81-968181-3-5
© 2023 Suhana Rossi. All rights reserved.
Images Source: Pixbay: (https://pixabay.com/)
All images' rights belong to their respective owners.
Disclaimer: The author and publisher disclaim all liability for accuracy, loss, or damage arising from the use of this travel guide; users are urged to independently verify information and prioritize personal safety.

Catalog

The Enchanting Beauty and Rich Historical Legacy

Amidst the countless destinations that the world boasts about, lies a hidden gem called the Harz region in Germany. This captivating place offers a harmonious blend of pristine natural landscapes and historical treasures that will leave you spellbound. Nestled right in the heart of Germany, Harz invites you to embark on a journey of exploration, where charming towns and lush green hills echo with the whispers of an intriguing past.

Wernigerode: A Fairytale Town with Timber-Framed Delights

Wernigerode is like stepping into a fairytale with its quaint timber-framed houses and enchanting cobbled streets. This town acts as a gateway to the cultural riches that Harz has to offer. The Wernigerode Castle, perched majestically on a hilltop, stands as a medieval masterpiece that captures the imagination. As you wander through its picturesque Old Town, complete with a vibrant market square, you'll find yourself immersed in history and captivated by charming architecture.

Quedlinburg: Where Time Comes to Life

Quedlinburg is more than just another UNESCO World Heritage site; it's a living testament to medieval history. Its well-preserved timber-framed houses and the towering Collegiate Church of St. Servatius transport you back in time to an era long gone. Stroll through its narrow alleys, and every step will resonate with echoes from centuries past.

Goslar: A Blend of Mining Legacy and Imperial Grandeur

Goslar seamlessly blends its mining heritage with imperial grandeur, making it yet another UNESCO gem in Harz region. The Rammelsberg Mines and Goslar's Old Town adorned with half-timbered houses provide glimpses into both its rich mining history and its significant role during the Holy Roman Empire.

Harz National Park: Nature's Symphony in Full Bloom

Harz National Park, a sprawling wilderness, invites nature enthusiasts to witness the symphony created by its diverse landscapes. From dense forests to hidden waterfalls and the majestic Brocken, Harz's highest peak offering panoramic views that stretch as far as the eye can see, every corner of the national park is a testament to nature's artistry.

Gastronomic Delights: Unveiling the Flavors of Harz Cuisine

Satisfy your taste buds with the local culinary delights that Harz has to offer. From hearty mountain stews to delicate pastries, each dish carries within it a reflection of the region's rich culinary heritage. Indulge in these mouthwatering specialties at charming gasthofs where warm hospitality awaits alongside flavors that will leave you craving for more.

Adventure Awaits: Embrace the Great Outdoors

While Harz is known for its historical charm, it also beckons adventurers with its array of outdoor escapades. Whether it's cycling through the breathtaking Harz Mountains, exploring the mystical Teufelsmauer (Devil's Wall), or discovering serenity on tranquil lakeshores, this region offers diverse experiences for every nature lover.

In Harz, every cobblestone has a story to tell and every forest trail whispers secrets from long ago. So take your time, immerse yourself in this vibrant cultural tapestry, and let Harz unveil its treasures - an exquisite harmony of history, nature, and unforgettable moments.

1. Wernigerode Castle:

Wernigerode Castle, situated above the town since the Middle Ages, has a rich history of transformation. Initially built as a fortress in the 12th century, it later transformed into a Renaissance-style residence during the 16th century. Throughout the centuries, this castle has witnessed wars and undergone renovations, becoming an emblem of regional power. Nowadays, visitors have the opportunity to explore its lavish chambers that tell tales of medieval and Renaissance history. Additionally, the castle's towers provide breathtaking panoramic views of the Harz landscapes.

Here are some key attractions you shouldn't miss when visiting Wernigerode Castle: immerse yourself in the opulence of its rooms, marvel at the impressive Knights' Hall, and delve into centuries-spanning exhibits at the Castle Museum.

For optimal weather conditions to explore both the castle and its gardens, it is recommended to visit during spring and summer.

The opening hours for Wernigerode Castle are from 10:00 AM to 6:00 PM every day.

If you need further information or want to plan your visit in advance, you can contact them at +49 3943 553673 or visit their [official website](https://www.schloss-wernigerode.de/en/).

2. Brocken:

The Brocken, the highest peak in Harz, has an enchanting past filled with folklore and natural splendor. In German mythology, it is known as the "Blocksberg" and was believed to be a gathering spot for witches on Walpurgis Night. This majestic mountain also played a significant role during the Cold War as it was located along the Iron Curtain. With its blend of mythological and geopolitical history, the Brocken is a captivating destination.

Here are some of its main attractions: panoramic views that will leave you breathless, a scenic railway called the Brocken Railway, and the Harz National Park Visitor Center where you can learn more about this fascinating place.

To make the most of your visit, consider coming in summer for clear views or during winter when the landscape transforms into a snowy wonderland.

For more information or to plan your trip, you can contact Harzer Schmalspurbahnen at +49 3943 5580 or visit [National Park Visitor Center's website](https://www.nationalpark-harz.de/en/).

3. Quedlinburg Old Town:

Quedlinburg's Old Town is steeped in rich history, spanning over a thousand years since its establishment in 922. Its medieval timber-framed houses and cobblestone streets have preserved the town's enchanting medieval allure. The Collegiate Church of St. Servatius, recognized as a UNESCO World Heritage site, has served as a spiritual hub since the 10th century. Quedlinburg's architectural marvels vividly showcase its historical journey, transforming it into a living museum that encapsulates both the medieval and Renaissance periods.

If you're planning to visit, make sure to explore key attractions such as St. Servatius Church, Market Square, and the Fachwerkmuseum (Timber Frame Museum). The town welcomes visitors all year round, with an especially magical experience during the Christmas Market in December.

For more information and assistance, you can reach out to Quedlinburg Tourist Information at +49 3946 9057-0 or visit their official tourism website at [Tourism Website](https://www.quedlinburg.de/en/).

4. Rammelsberg Mines:

The Rammelsberg Mines, a UNESCO World Heritage site, are a testament to the rich mining history of Goslar. With over a millennium of operation, these mines played a significant role in the region's economic and cultural growth by providing valuable ore. The well-preserved structures, machinery, and tunnels provide insight into the challenges and advancements of medieval mining techniques.

If you're planning to visit, make sure to check out the Mining Museum, Roeder Stollen Mine, and the historic mining equipment - they're definitely worth exploring. The best time to visit is during spring to autumn when outdoor tours are available.

For more information or inquiries about your visit, you can reach out to the Rammelsberg Mines Visitor Center at +49 5321 750-122 or visit their [Official Website](https://www.rammelsberg.de/en/).

The Goslar Imperial Palace, an awe-inspiring architectural masterpiece dating back to the 11th century, stands as a symbol of the immense imperial authority wielded by the Holy Roman Empire. Once serving as a prestigious residence for German emperors, this magnificent palace witnessed numerous historic events, most notably imperial assemblies. Immerse yourself in the opulence and grandeur of medieval times at the Kaiserpfalz Museum, where captivating tales unfold, offering valuable insights into the political and cultural milieu of the empire at its pinnacle.

Discover key attractions within this remarkable complex, including the esteemed Kaiserpfalz Museum, where history comes alive before your eyes. Step into the Throne Room and feel a sense of reverence as you contemplate the weighty decisions made within these hallowed walls. Marvel at the exquisite craftsmanship and spiritual significance of the Chapel of St. Ulrich.

No matter when you choose to visit this extraordinary site, there is always something to captivate your interest. While summer brings special events that further enhance your experience, Goslar Imperial Palace welcomes visitors throughout the year.

For more information and assistance in planning your visit to this historical gem, reach out to the helpful staff at Kaiserpfalz Visitor Center by calling +49 5321 31125 or visit their [official website](https://www.goslar.de/en/).

6. Bode Gorge (Bodetal):

Bode Gorge, a mesmerizing natural wonder shaped by the relentless flow of the Bode River over countless years, holds a captivating history that mirrors the ancient landscapes it adorns. This breathtaking gorge not only served as a vital passage for traders and pilgrims in bygone eras but continues to beckon adventurous souls to embark on an enchanting journey through its winding trails. As you traverse this timeless terrain, you'll find yourself surrounded by majestic cliffs and vibrant greenery, seamlessly bridging the gap between the present and the geological past.

Now, let's delve into some of its key attractions that add an extra touch of allure to this already spellbinding destination. The Hexentanzplatz offers a mystical ambiance that will transport you to another realm, while the Rosstrappe unveils its own mystique with legends and folklore intertwined with its rugged beauty. And of course, no visit would be complete without exploring the numerous hiking trails that weave through this picturesque landscape.

To truly immerse yourself in the splendor of Bode Gorge, plan your visit during spring or summer when nature is at its most resplendent. During these seasons, lush greenery blankets every corner, creating a visual symphony that will leave you awestruck.

For more information and assistance in planning your trip to this extraordinary destination, feel free to reach out to Harzer Tourismusverband at +49 3941 53-4000 or visit their informative website [Harz Tourism Website](https://en.harzinfo.de/). They will be delighted to help you make your journey even more memorable.

Embark on an unforgettable adventure through Bode Gorge - where time stands still and nature's grandeur unfolds before your eyes.

7. Thale Hexentanzplatz:

The Hexentanzplatz, also known as the Witches' Dance Floor, holds a fascinating history intertwined with pagan ceremonies. In times of old, this plateau was revered as a sacred location where witches would gather. Positioned above the breathtaking Bode Gorge, the Hexentanzplatz not only offers picturesque vistas but also serves as a conduit to the ancient beliefs and customs of the region.

If you're planning a visit, there are several key attractions to explore. The Witches' Dance Floor itself is a must-see, along with the nearby Animal Park and an exhilarating cable car ride. To make the most of your trip, it's best to plan for a visit during spring to autumn when outdoor activities are in full swing.

For further information or assistance, you can reach out to Thale Tourist Information at +49 3947 78207 or visit their website at [Thale Website](https://www.thale.de/).

8. Stolberg:

Stolberg is a town that exudes medieval charm, tracing its roots back to the 12th century. Once a Free Imperial City, it thrived thanks to mining and trade. The marketplace, surrounded by beautifully preserved half-timbered houses, serves as a testament to the vibrant medieval markets and festivities that once took place here. Stolberg's rich history is evident in the intricate details of its historic buildings, offering an immersive experience for visitors.

If you're planning a trip to Stolberg, there are several key attractions worth exploring. The marketplace itself is a must-see, along with the impressive St. Martini Church and the picturesque half-timbered houses.

To make the most of your visit, consider coming during the summer when you can take part in outdoor events and festivals that bring the town to life with excitement and celebration.

For more information about Stolberg and its attractions, you can reach out to Stolberg Tourist Information at +49 39454 288 or visit their website [Stolberg Website](https://www.stolberg-erzgebirge.de/).

9. Kyffhäuser Monument:

The Kyffhäuser Monument, which was built in the late 19th century, is a historical tribute to Emperor William I. Its location on top of the Kyffhäuser mountain holds great historical significance due to the legends surrounding Emperor Frederick I (Barbarossa) and his anticipated resurrection. This monumental structure not only serves as an homage to the emperor but also provides awe-inspiring panoramic views of the surrounding landscapes.

Some of its key attractions include the breathtaking panoramic views, the mysterious Barbarossa Cave, and the memorial hall. To fully appreciate these attractions, it is recommended to visit during the spring to autumn seasons when clear views are guaranteed.

For more information, you can contact Kyffhäuser Tourist Information at +49 34671 62207 or visit their website at [Kyffhäuser Website](https://www.kyffhaeuserland.de/).

10. Bad Harzburg:

Bad Harzburg, a charming spa town with a rich history dating back to the 19th century, has always been closely tied to its natural mineral springs and wellness culture. Over the years, it has gained popularity among nobility and statesmen as a renowned health resort. The town's commitment to providing visitors with ultimate relaxation and rejuvenation is evident in its iconic Burgberg Cable Car, which has been in operation since 1929.

If you're planning a visit to Bad Harzburg, make sure to check out some of its key attractions. Take a ride on the Burgberg Cable Car for breathtaking views and an unforgettable experience. Indulge in some pampering at the Sole-Therme Spa, where you can unwind and rejuvenate your body and mind. For nature enthusiasts, don't miss the Baumwipfelpfad treetop walk that offers a unique perspective of the surrounding beauty.

Bad Harzburg is a year-round destination with something to offer in every season. While summer is perfect for outdoor activities like hiking or exploring the picturesque landscapes, other seasons also have their own charm.

For more information about Bad Harzburg and planning your trip, you can reach out to Bad Harzburg Tourist Information at Tel: +49 5322 75330 or visit their official website [Bad Harzburg Website](https://www.bad-harzburg.de/en/). They will be more than happy to assist you with any inquiries or help you make the most of your visit.

11. Teufelsmauer (Devil's Wall):

The Teufelsmauer, also known as the Devil's Wall, is a captivating rock formation that holds a rich history and is surrounded by local legends. Carved over time by the erosion of sandstone, it has intrigued people for centuries. According to folklore, the wall has supernatural origins, with stories depicting the devil constructing it overnight. This site holds great historical significance, blending geological processes with imaginative narratives from local folklore.

One of its main attractions are the hiking trails that wind along the rock formation, offering breathtaking panoramic views. It is best to visit during the spring to autumn seasons when hiking conditions are ideal. For more information and inquiries about visiting this enchanting place, you can reach out to Harzer Tourismusverband at +49 3941 53-4000 or visit their [Harz Tourism Website](https://en.harzinfo.de/).

12. Hahnenklee:

Hahnenklee, with its origins dating back to the 17th century, has a fascinating past deeply rooted in mining. Originally established as a mining village, it thrived during the prosperous era of the Harz mining industry. A true testament to the region's cultural heritage is the iconic Stave Church, which was meticulously crafted in 1908. Today, Hahnenklee not only serves as a historical treasure but also beckons outdoor enthusiasts and cultural aficionados throughout the year.

Here are some of the noteworthy attractions in Hahnenklee: The Stave Church, an architectural marvel that captivates visitors; the Bocksberg Cable Car, offering breathtaking views; and the Bocksbergalm, an idyllic spot to unwind.

No matter what time of year you choose to visit Hahnenklee, there's always something to enjoy. In winter, skiing enthusiasts can hit the slopes while other outdoor activities await during other seasons. To plan your trip or gather more information about this enchanting destination, you can reach out to Hahnenklee Tourist Information at +49 5325 268 or visit their website [Hahnenklee Website](https://www.hahnenklee.de/).

13. Drei Annen Hohne:

Drei Annen Hohne holds a significant place in the history of the Brocken Railway, dating back to the late 19th century. This junction not only served as a starting point for picturesque hikes but also acted as a meeting point for multiple railway lines, making it an essential hub in the region's transportation landscape. To this day, the Harzer Schmalspurbahnen Museum located at the station stands as a testament to the rich heritage of narrow-gauge railways in the Harz area.

If you're planning a visit, some key attractions include the Brocken Railway station itself, which is steeped in history and charm. The surrounding hiking trails offer breathtaking views and an opportunity to immerse yourself in nature's beauty. And don't forget to explore the Harzer Schmalspurbahnen Museum, where you can delve deeper into the fascinating world of narrow-gauge railways.

No matter when you plan your trip, Drei Annen Hohne welcomes visitors throughout the year. However, if you're looking for maximum activity and vibrancy, summer is undoubtedly the peak season.

For more information or inquiries about your visit, you can reach out to Harzer Schmalspurbahnen at +49 3943 5580 or visit their website [Harzer Schmalspurbahnen](https://www.hsb-wr.de/).

The Oberharzer Wasserregal is an incredible UNESCO World Heritage site that showcases historic water management systems spanning from the 16th to the 19th centuries. These ingenious systems were initially developed to support the mining industry and played a crucial role in powering mills and facilitating ore transportation. For a detailed exploration of the technological marvels of the Wasserregal, make sure to visit the Clausthal-Zellerfeld Mining Museum. Alongside this, you can also enjoy attractions like Huttaler Widerwaage and explore the beautiful hiking trails in the area. To make the most of your visit, plan your trip during spring to autumn when you can fully immerse yourself in outdoor exploration. For more information or to contact Oberharzer Bergwerksmuseum, you can reach them at +49 5323 98940 or visit their website [here](https://www.wasserregal.de/en/).

15. Königshütte:

Königshütte, a former ironworks complex dating back to the 19th century, holds great significance in the industrial history of the Harz region. Its story is vividly portrayed at the Ironworks Museum, which traces the development of the industry and its profound socio-economic impact on the neighboring villages.

Königshütte stands as a remarkable testament to the region's industrial prowess during a time of immense transformation.

The attractions that make Königshütte truly captivating include the Ironworks Museum itself, along with its scenic hiking trails and picturesque village setting. Whether you choose to visit in summer for special events or any other time of year, Königshütte offers an enriching experience.

For more information about visiting Königshütte, you can reach out to the friendly staff at Königshütte Tourist Information by calling +49 39457 67690. Additionally, you can explore their website at [Königshütte Website](https://www.koenigshuette-harz.de/).

16. Braunlage:

Braunlage, a vibrant town with deep roots in mining and forestry, has transformed into a sought-after destination for outdoor enthusiasts. The Wurmberg Cable Car, which has been in operation since 1922, provides convenient transportation for both locals and visitors. Today, Braunlage maintains its historical allure while catering to modern interests, creating a dynamic hub that offers both relaxation and adventure.

When it comes to key attractions, visitors can enjoy the Wurmberg Cable Car, explore the Braunlage Witches' Trail, and immerse themselves in the lively town center.

No matter the season, Braunlage is a year-round destination with winter skiing as an added attraction. Whether you're seeking historical exploration or thrilling outdoor adventures, these attractions guarantee an unforgettable experience in the captivating Harz region.

For more information and to plan your visit, you can contact Braunlage Tourist Information at +49 5520 90100 or visit their website at [Braunlage Website](https://www.braunlage.de/en/).

Harz Heritage Discovery - 2 Weeks

Unveiling the Treasures of History
Embark on an enthralling voyage through the cultural and historical marvels of the Harz region.
Days 1 - 3: Wernigerode
Begin your adventure in Wernigerode, a town brimming with medieval allure. Immerse yourself in the grandeur of Wernigerode Castle, witness its Renaissance transformation, and meander through the cobblestone streets of the Old Town. Don't forget to visit the captivating Wernigerode Town Hall and soak in the lively atmosphere of the vibrant market square.
Days 4 - 6: Quedlinburg
Next, venture into Quedlinburg's UNESCO-listed Old Town. Delve into over a thousand years of history as you explore the charming half-timbered houses and pay a visit to the awe-inspiring Collegiate Church of St. Servatius. Immerse yourself in the rich tapestry of culture that weaves this medieval town together.
Days 7 - 9: Goslar
Journey into Goslar's historical heart. The Rammelsberg Mines, a UNESCO World Heritage site, beckon with tales of mining glory from centuries past. Marvel at Goslar Imperial Palace, an architectural gem dating back to the 11th century, and take leisurely strolls along picturesque streets adorned with impeccably preserved medieval structures.
Days 10 - 12: Harz National Park
Immerse yourself in nature's wonders within Harz National Park. Embark on invigorating hikes through scenic trails like Bode Gorge, where you can revel in diverse flora and fauna while breathing in pure mountain air. Discover hidden gems nestled along these well-marked paths, offering tranquil moments of respite from the bustling world.
Days 13 - 15: Thale and Hexentanzplatz

Conclude your journey in Thale, home to the mystical Hexentanzplatz. Unearth the folklore and legends that enshroud this plateau as you indulge in a cable car ride for breathtaking panoramic views. Explore the surrounding landscapes, ensuring a perfect finale to your Harz Heritage Discovery.

Harz Arts and Nature Trail - 2 Weeks

Immersing in Artistic Legacies and Natural Splendors
Embark on a voyage that seamlessly intertwines the artistic heritage of the Harz region with its awe-inspiring natural landscapes.
Days 1 - 3: Stolberg
Commence your exploration in Stolberg, an enchanting medieval gem dating back to the 12th century. Wander through its historic marketplace, framed by meticulously preserved half-timbered houses. Stolberg sets the stage for your artistic and natural odyssey with its timeless charm.
Days 4 - 6: Hahnenklee
Next, venture into the picturesque village of Hahnenklee, where history harmonizes with nature. Pay a visit to the iconic wooden Stave Church and ascend on a cable car ride to Bocksberg for awe-inspiring panoramic vistas. Immerse yourself in the artistic allure and natural splendor that define this captivating destination.
Days 7 - 9: Oberharzer Wasserregal
Explore Oberharzer Wasserregal, a UNESCO World Heritage site showcasing ingenious water management systems that stand as testaments to centuries-old engineering brilliance. Unveil the fascinating history of mining as you marvel at historic water channels and structures. For deeper insights into this industrial legacy, visit Clausthal-Zellerfeld Mining Museum.
Days 10 - 12: Braunlage and Wurmberg
Experience the vibrant town of Braunlage, a gateway to the Wurmberg ski resort. Delight in a plethora of outdoor activities, from exhilarating skiing in winter to invigorating hikes in summer. Ascend the Wurmberg Cable Car for awe-inspiring views and savor the lively ambiance of this multifaceted town.
Days 13 - 15: Lakes and Nature Retreat

Conclude your journey with a serene lakeside retreat at either Lake St. Andreasberg or the enchanting Oderteich Reservoir. Immerse yourself in nature's tranquility, reflecting upon the harmonious fusion of art and natural wonders that define the essence of the Harz region.

Exploring the Mystical Harz National Park through Hiking

Embarking on a hiking adventure in the Harz National Park is like stepping into a pristine expanse of ancient forests, cascading waterfalls, and meandering trails. The Selketalstieg trail, with its historic charm, is waiting to be explored. And if you're up for a challenge, don't miss the opportunity to ascend the Brocken, the highest peak in the region. The best time to experience this immersive hiking journey is from April to June when wildflowers paint a kaleidoscope of colors across the landscape.

Mountain Biking Thrills in Braunlage and along the Harz Witches' Trail

For those seeking an adrenaline rush on two wheels, Braunlage offers thrilling mountain biking opportunities. Navigating through dense forests and conquering challenging terrains will surely get your heart racing. Another exciting option is exploring the Harz Witches' Trail, where enchanting landscapes and historic sites await you at every turn. With trails catering to both beginners and seasoned bikers, there's something for everyone. And let's not forget about autumn when crisp air and vibrant foliage add an extra layer of excitement to mountain biking in the Harz.

Winter Sports Wonderland in Braunlage, Wurmberg, and Hahnenklee

When winter arrives and blankets the Harz region in snow, it transforms into a haven for winter sports enthusiasts. Braunlage,

Wurmberg, and Hahnenklee offer exhilarating downhill skiing experiences that will leave you craving more adrenaline. Cross-country skiing enthusiasts can explore well-groomed trails that crisscross the picturesque Harz National Park. The serene landscapes draped in snow create a magical backdrop for unforgettable winter adventures. December to March is undoubtedly prime time for snowy escapades.

Rock Climbing and Via Ferrata Adventures in Okertalsperre

If you're a fan of rock climbing, the rugged cliffs of Okertalsperre will be your playground. Here, you'll find challenging rock faces suitable for both beginners and seasoned climbers. Single-pitch routes provide a great starting point for those new to the sport, while multipitch ascents offer a thrilling challenge for experienced climbers. For a unique twist on rock climbing, try the Okertalsperre Via Ferrata, which combines high-altitude hiking with vertical thrills. The stunning vistas that await you at the top are worth every bit of effort.

Water-Based Fun in Okertalsperre Reservoir and along the Innerste River

While the Harz region may not have vast coastlines, it surprises visitors with its water-based adventures. Kayaking through the serene waters of the Okertalsperre reservoir is an experience like no other. Surrounded by lush forests and dramatic cliffs, you'll feel completely immersed in nature's beauty. If you're seeking more excitement, head to the Innerste River for white-water paddling during the spring thaw. And if tranquility is what you crave, stand-up paddleboarding on Oker Lake is a perfect choice.

Paragliding: Taking Flight from Brocken Summit

For those who dream of soaring above it all, paragliding adventures launched from the Brocken summit offer an unparalleled experience. Imagine panoramic views stretching as far as your eyes can see and feeling like you're floating amidst the vast expanse of Harz skies. Tandem flights provide an accessible introduction to this thrilling activity, allowing adventurers to enjoy all the freedom that comes with flying.

Choosing Your Adventure Time

- Spring (April to June): This is when nature awakens and blooms with wildflowers—ideal for hiking.
- Summer (July and August): The perfect time for mountain biking enthusiasts, rock climbers seeking new heights, and water activity lovers.
- Winter (December to March): The prime season for skiing, snowboarding, and all kinds of winter sports.
The Harz region is not just a playground for outdoor enthusiasts; it's a diverse landscape embedded with rich cultural history. Throughout the changing seasons, from scaling rocky heights to gliding through the air or navigating snowy slopes, the Harz invites adventurers to uncover its exhilarating offerings.

Geological Foundations
The history of the Harz region is deeply rooted in its geological formations, which are responsible for its unique topography and natural beauty. Over millions of years, the Harz Mountains were formed during a period of intense tectonic activity called the Variscan orogeny. This collision of ancient continents resulted in the uplift of the Harz, creating rugged mountains, dense forests, and pristine valleys.

Throughout the Paleozoic era, various geological processes such as erosion and sedimentation shaped the diverse landscapes we see today in the Harz. The region's abundant mineral deposits, particularly ore-bearing rocks, played a significant role in human settlement and economic development over centuries. The geological history of the Harz not only contributes to its scenic beauty but also provides a backdrop for the rich human narratives that have unfolded over millennia.

Prehistoric Inhabitants and Celtic Influence
As these geological processes shaped the Harz region, prehistoric communities began to inhabit it. Archaeological evidence suggests that Neanderthals inhabited the area during the Middle Paleolithic period, with remnants of their tools and artifacts discovered in caves and rock shelters. However, it was during later periods, notably the Bronze Age, that human presence became more pronounced in the Harz.

The Celts, an influential Iron Age culture, left a lasting impact on the Harz region. Evidence of Celtic settlements and artifacts has been unearthed, showcasing their advanced metallurgical skills and cultural practices. The Celts were drawn to this area because of its abundant natural resources, particularly metal deposits. This early interaction between human communities and the region's geological wealth set the stage for subsequent historical developments.

Medieval Transformations and Mining Boom

The medieval period witnessed significant transformations in both socio-economic landscape and cultural identity within the Harz region. One pivotal development was mining activities taking off which marked beginning as crucial mining center not just for Europe but globally too.The mountains of Harz were a source of silver, copper, lead, and other precious metals. This mining industry contributed to the wealth of local rulers and fostered the growth of vibrant mining towns.

In the 10th century, Holy Roman Emperor Otto the Great established mines in the Harz region, highlighting its economic and political importance. In the following centuries, the Harz Mining Association emerged as a powerful guild that regulated mining activities and played a key role in shaping regional governance. Towns like Goslar and Clausthal-Zellerfeld thrived as mining hubs, with their medieval architecture reflecting the prosperity brought by mining endeavors.

The mining boom also led to technological advancements such as water-powered ore mills and improved mining regulations. However, economic success was not without challenges, often resulting in conflicts over mining rights among different stakeholders. Despite these complexities, the medieval period laid a foundation for the enduring association between the Harz region and its rich cultural heritage shaped by mining.

Renaissance, Reformation, and Cultural Significance

The Renaissance and Reformation eras brought significant changes to both cultural dynamics and religious landscape within the Harz region. In the 16th century, Protestantism spread across Europe with strongholds emerging in places like Harz. The mining towns played a central role in this religious transformation as miners actively participated in spreading Protestant ideas.

During this period of cultural resurgence known as Renaissance ,the Harz experienced its own renaissance.The towns flourished with impressive timber-framed houses,churches,guild halls which showcased prosperity derived from successfulmining operations.Notable examples include Wernigerode's market square & intricately designed town hall in Quedlinburg which reflected architectural finesse of that era.

The cultural richness extended beyond architecture to literature & folklore too.The Brothers Grimm who are renowned for their collection of fairy tales drew inspiration from enchanting landscapes& medieval charm found withinHarz region.Dense forests,misty mountains and ancient castles provided the perfect backdrop for timeless tales such as "Snow White" and "Hansel and Gretel."

Throughout the centuries that followed, the Harz remained a sanctuary for culture, drawing in artists, writers, and intellectuals alike. The breathtaking beauty of the region's natural landscapes served as a wellspring of inspiration for romantic poets, forever immortalizing the Harz in works of literature and art. This vibrant cultural legacy is still palpable today, evident in the meticulously preserved historic towns, artistic expressions that abound, and the timeless appeal of the Harz as a destination where history, culture, and natural wonders harmoniously converge.

Here are some amazing hotels in Germany that you should definitely check out:
1. Hotel Der Achtermann
- Located at Rosentorstraße 20, 38640 Goslar, Germany
- Contact them at +49 5321 7030
- Visit their website: [Hotel Der Achtermann](https://www.achtermann-goslar.de/)
2. Maritim Berghotel Braunlage
- Situated at Am Pfaffenstieg, 38700 Braunlage, Germany
- Give them a call at +49 5520 8070
- Check out their website: [Maritim Berghotel Braunlage](https://www.maritim.com/en/hotels/germany/berghotel-braunlage)
3. Romantik Hotel Gebhardtwald Schierke
- Found at Am Gerneberg 1, 38879 Schierke, Germany
- Reach them at +49 39455 8090
- Explore their website: [Romantik Hotel Gebhardtwald Schierke](https://www.romantikhotel-gebhardtwald.de/)
4. Travel Charme Gothisches Haus
- Located at Marktplatz 2, 38855 Wernigerode, Germany
- Contact them at +49 3943 9410
- Visit their website: [Travel Charme Gothisches Haus](https://www.gothisches-haus.de/)
5. Landhaus "Zu den Rothen Forellen"
- Address: Marktplatz 2, Wernigerode, Germany
- Telephone Number : +49 3943 9410
- Website :[Landhaus "Zu den Rothen Forellen"](https://www.rotheforelle.de/)
6. Hotel Waldschlösschen Schierke
- Located at Brockenweg 1, 38879 Schierke, Germany
- Contact them at +49 39455 8380
- Visit their website: [Hotel Waldschlösschen Schierke](https://www.waldschloesschen-schierke.de/)
7. H+ Hotel Goslar

- Situated at Baßgeige 27, 38644 Goslar, Germany
- Give them a call at +49 5321 70090
- Check out their website: [H+ Hotel Goslar](https://www.h-hotels.com/de/hplus/hotels/hplus-hotel-goslar)
8. Hotel Schlossvilla Derenburg
- Found at Halberstädter Str. 1, 38895 Derenburg, Germany
- Reach them at +49 3943 5310
- Explore their website: [Hotel Schlossvilla Derenburg](https://www.schlossvilla-derenburg.de/)
9. Hotel Fürstenhof Wernigerode
Address: Pfarrstraße 41, Wernigerode, Germany
- Telephone Number : +49 3943 5530
- Website :[Hotel Fürstenhof Wernigerode](https://www.fuerstenhof-wernigerode.de/)
10. Ringhotel Weißer Hirsch
Address: Marktplatz5-6 ,Halberstadt, Germany
- Telephone Number : +49 39415510
- Website :[Ringhotel Weißer Hirsch](https://www.weisserhirsch.de/)
These hotels offer excellent accommodations and services for a memorable stay. Make sure to visit their websites for more information and booking details.

When planning your trip to the captivating landscapes of the Harz region, it is essential to understand the visa and residency regulations to ensure a seamless and legal visit. Here is a detailed overview tailored specifically for travelers:

1. European Citizens and Schengen Agreement:

- If you are from a European country that is part of the Schengen Agreement, you can freely enter the Harz region using a valid identity card or passport.

2. Visa Exemptions for Selected Countries:

- Citizens from 28 non-EU countries, including Australia, Brazil, Canada, Israel, Japan, New Zealand, and the USA (to name a few), do not need a visa for tourist stays of up to 90 days. It's important to note that visa requirements may vary if you plan on extending your trip to the UK and Ireland.

3. Visas for Non-EU and Non-Schengen Nationals:

- Non-EU and non-Schengen nationals who plan on staying in the Harz region for more than 90 days or have purposes other than tourism (such as work or study) may require specific visas.

- For accurate and up-to-date information on visa requirements, it is advisable to consult the official website www.esteri.it/visti/home_eng.asp or contact an Italian consulate.

4. Residence and Work for EU Citizens:

- EU citizens have the privilege of residing and working in the Harz region without needing any permits. However, after three months of stay, it is mandatory to register at the local municipal registry office. You may be asked to provide evidence of employment or sufficient financial means.

5. Permanent Residence for Non-EU Foreign Citizens:

- Non-EU foreign citizens who have legally resided in the Harz region for five continuous years can apply for permanent residence status.

6. Permesso di Soggiorno (Permit to Stay):

- Non-EU citizens planning to stay at a fixed address for more than one week should obtain a 'permesso di soggiorno' or permit to stay from the local police station.

- Tourists staying in hotels are usually exempt from this requirement.

- Obtaining a 'permesso di soggiorno' is necessary for study, work, or long-term residence. The application process, which requires specific documentation, can be found on www.poliziadistato.it under 'Foreign nationals.'

7. Study Visas:

- Non-EU citizens who wish to study in the Harz region, whether at a university or language school, must apply for a study visa at the nearest Italian embassy or consulate.

- The documentation typically includes proof of enrollment, fee payments, and financial means to support yourself during your studies.

- Study visas are aligned with the duration of enrollment and can be renewed within the Harz region by demonstrating ongoing enrollment and sufficient financial support.

By understanding these visa and residency intricacies, you can ensure a smooth and compliant stay in the enchanting Harz region. Always refer to official sources for the latest requirements and regulations to make your exploration of this beautiful locale hassle-free and within legal boundaries.

When it comes to traveling to the breathtaking Harz region in Germany, there are numerous transportation choices available that cater to travelers from all around the world. Whether you prefer air travel, land routes, or even sea exploration, the Harz ensures seamless connectivity to its captivating destinations.

Taking to the Skies:

The Harz region can be easily accessed through several airports, with Hannover Airport and Leipzig/Halle Airport serving as primary gateways. These airports offer both domestic and international flights, providing a well-connected journey for travelers. Renowned airlines like Lufthansa and Eurowings operate regular services for added convenience.

Entering the Region:

European Union citizens can conveniently use their national identity cards for entry into the Harz region. However, individuals from other nationalities typically require a valid passport. It's important to note that carrying identification is mandatory according to local law and essential for police registration at accommodations.

Navigating by Land:

The road and rail networks in the Harz region seamlessly connect it with neighboring countries. Key border crossings include:
- Germany to Austria: Travelers can embark on a picturesque journey from Garmisch-Partenkirchen to Innsbruck via A95/E533.
- Germany to Czech Republic: Options abound for crossing from Dresden to Prague via E55/D8.

Affordable Bus Travel:

While bus services may not offer the same level of frequency or comfort as trains, they present an economical means of transportation. Eurolines connects major cities in the region, making it accessible for budget-conscious travelers seeking adventure.

Exploring by Car and Motorcycle:

For those coming from Continental Europe:

- It is important that vehicles crossing borders display their country of registration's nationality plate.
- Proof of vehicle ownership and third-party insurance are essential requirements. EU-registered vehicles generally have sufficient coverage with their home country insurance.
- The Harz region's scenic roads are a haven for motorcycle enthusiasts, particularly during the summer months.

Efficient Train Travel:

Germany's extensive railway network ensures excellent connectivity to the Harz region. Regular train services link the area with neighboring countries, providing efficient and eco-friendly travel options.

For travelers from Continental Europe:

- The European Rail Timetable is a valuable resource for comprehensive train schedules.
- Reservations on international trains are advisable and sometimes mandatory.
- Certain trains even offer transportation options for private cars.
For travelers from the UK:
- Eurostar high-velocity trains provide seamless connections from London to Paris or Brussels, offering an easy way to reach the Harz region.

Sea Adventures:

While the Harz region itself is landlocked, travelers can still indulge in sea travel by exploring ferry options in nearby cities. Ferry services connect Germany with Scandinavian countries, providing an alternative and scenic mode of transportation.

For detailed ferry schedules and services, websites such as [traghettionline.com](https://www.traghettionline.com) and [ferries.gr](https://www.ferries.gr) offer comprehensive information that can assist you in planning your journey.

In conclusion, the captivating Harz region offers a diverse range of transportation options to ensure that every traveler can find a suitable and enjoyable way to reach this picturesque destination.

Discover the vibrant local events and festivals in the Harz region that will captivate your senses throughout the year. Immerse yourself in the rich culture and natural beauty while enjoying a wide range of festivities. Let's dive into some of these remarkable experiences:

1. Harz National Park Anniversary Celebration:

  - Date: Every June

  - Season: Embrace the warmth of summer

  - Join the jubilations as we commemorate the establishment of Harz National Park during June. This annual celebration offers a perfect blend of eco-friendly activities, guided nature walks, and informative programs that shed light on our conservation efforts. Get ready to immerse yourself in the breathtaking beauty of this park while expanding your knowledge about sustainable practices.

2. Walpurgis Night:

  - Date: April 30th

  - Season: Embrace springtime enchantment

  - Experience an evening filled with mystical wonders during Walpurgis Night, which takes place on April 30th. The Harz region comes alive with captivating costumed processions, mesmerizing bonfires, and live music that fills the air. Allow yourself to be transported into a world steeped in folklore traditions amidst blooming trees and budding nature.

3. Harz Narrow Gauge Railways Steam Festival:

  - Date: Every August

  - Season: Late summer delights

  - All aboard for an unforgettable journey through time at the Harz Narrow Gauge Railways Steam Festival held annually in August. As late summer paints its vibrant hues across our landscapes, historic steam locomotives take center stage, traversing picturesque routes amidst awe-inspiring views of the Harz Mountains. Prepare to be captivated by both our rich history and stunning natural scenery.

4. Christmas Markets in the Harz Towns:

- Date: Late November to December
- Season: Embrace the warmth of winter
- Immerse yourself in the magical ambiance of the holiday season at the enchanting Christmas markets spread across various Harz towns. From late November to December, our region transforms into a true winter wonderland, adorned with festive decorations and illuminated by the warm glow of seasonal treats. Explore local crafts, indulge in traditional delicacies, and embrace the joyful spirit that fills every corner.

5. Brocken Marathon:
- Date: Every September
- Season: Embrace the early autumn breeze
- Lace up your running shoes and prepare for an invigorating challenge at the Brocken Marathon held annually in September. Whether you're conquering our highest peak or cheering on fellow participants, you'll be immersed in a dynamic atmosphere that fuels your passion for adventure. Let the early autumn colors inspire you as you embark on this thrilling journey through nature's marvels.

6. Harz Music Festival:
- Date: Throughout the year
- Season: Varied experiences await
- Indulge your senses in an exquisite blend of classical and contemporary music at the renowned Harz Music Festival. Throughout the year, this festival offers a diverse range of musical performances set against historic venues that exude charm and elegance. Allow yourself to be transported by captivating melodies as they harmonize with nature's ever-changing seasons.

7. Osterode Horse Parade:
- Date: Every July
- Season: Bask in summer splendor
- Prepare to be amazed by the captivating Osterode Horse Parade held annually in July, where equestrian traditions take center stage. Adorned horses accompanied by skilled riders create a vibrant spectacle that weaves through our streets, leaving spectators awestruck under the warm summer sun. Experience

this breathtaking display of grace and beauty amidst a backdrop of picturesque scenery.

8. Okertalsperre Fireworks Festival:
  - Date: Every August
  - Season: Late summer's magical allure
  - Prepare to be dazzled by the Okertalsperre Fireworks Festival held every August. As the sun sets, the night sky becomes a canvas adorned with a mesmerizing display of colors, perfectly complementing the scenic backdrop of the reservoir. Allow yourself to be enchanted by this captivating evening under a starlit sky, where moments of pure magic unfold before your eyes.

9. Goslar Medieval Christmas Market:
  - Date: Late November to December
  - Season: Embrace the enchantment of winter
  - Step back in time and immerse yourself in medieval charm at the Goslar Medieval Christmas Market, held from late November to December. Wander through cobblestone streets adorned with medieval-themed decorations as you explore stalls filled with traditional crafts and hearty culinary delights. Let this unique yuletide experience transport you to an era filled with wonder and warmth.

10. Herb Market in Wernigerode:
  - Date: Every May
  - Season: Embrace the vibrant hues of springtime
  - Embark on a sensory journey through herbs, spices, and natural remedies at the Herb Market in Wernigerode held annually in May. Spring sets the stage for this vibrant market where local herbalists and artisans come together to showcase their creations. Explore an array of fragrances, flavors, and healing traditions as you delve into this immersive experience that celebrates nature's abundance.

Immerse yourself in these remarkable local events and festivals that offer a tapestry of experiences throughout each season. Let their allure captivate your senses and create lasting memories amidst the breathtaking landscapes of Harz region

Immerse yourself in the breathtaking beauty of the Harz region by venturing into its diverse nature reserves and parks. From enchanting forests to picturesque mountain landscapes, these protected areas provide a sanctuary for nature enthusiasts and those who love outdoor adventures.

1. Harz National Park:

- Deep within the heart of the Harz Mountains lies the magnificent Harz National Park, a haven teeming with biodiversity. Embark on over 200 kilometers of hiking trails that will lead you through ancient woodlands, serene lakes, and up to the iconic Brocken summit. While admission is typically free, keep in mind that guided tours may have associated fees.

2. High Moorland Dohren and Stadtwald Bad Harzburg:

- Explore the unique ecosystem of High Moorland Dohren, where you'll encounter raised bogs and a rich variety of flora. For a more leisurely stroll, wander through Stadtwald Bad Harzburg, a municipal forest offering picturesque walking paths. Best of all, both destinations are accessible free of charge.

3. Okertalsperre Nature Reserve:

- Surrounding the Okertalsperre reservoir is the captivating Okertalsperre Nature Reserve. Follow hiking trails that hug the water's edge as you marvel at its scenic beauty. While admission is often free, please note that parking fees may apply.

4. Ilsetal Nature Reserve:

- Find tranquility in Ilsetal as you meander along its winding river and through its wooded slopes. Take your time exploring the reserve's trails while observing local wildlife in their natural habitat. Entrance to this enchanting sanctuary is usually free for visitors.

5. Bode Gorge (Bodetal):

- Prepare to be captivated by the natural wonder known as Bode Gorge, a deep and narrow valley carved by the meandering Bode River. Immerse yourself in the awe-inspiring beauty of towering cliffs as you hike through this breathtaking gorge. While access to the gorge itself is often freely available, certain attractions within it, such as the Hexentanzplatz, may have separate admission fees.

6. Wurmberg:

- As the highest peak in Lower Saxony, Wurmberg serves as a hub for outdoor enthusiasts seeking adventure. Explore the surrounding nature trails and indulge in panoramic views that will leave you in awe. The cost of experiencing Wurmberg varies depending on your chosen activities, such as cable car rides or ski passes.

7. Wildpark Christianental:

- Located near Wernigerode, Wildpark Christianental is a wildlife park that houses a variety of native species. Take a leisurely stroll along its well-designed trails while observing animals within spacious enclosures. Admission prices are reasonable, with special discounts available for children and families.

8. Eckerstausee Nature Reserve:

- Eckerstausee offers tranquility amidst lush landscapes surrounding its serene reservoir. Enjoy leisurely walks along scenic trails or perhaps even embark on a boat ride to further embrace the beauty of this enchanting reserve. Typically, admission to Eckerstausee is free; however additional activities may incur associated costs.

9. Selketal-Stieg:

- The Selketal-Stieg trail winds its way through the picturesque Selke Valley, enveloped by forests and meadows that are simply breathtaking to behold. Feel free to explore this captivating route at your own pace without any fees or charges.

10. Brocken Garden:

- Situated atop the Brocken summit lies the wondrous Brocken Garden where you can immerse yourself in alpine flora at its finest. Access to this magnificent garden may either be included in your Brocken Railway ticket or may require a separate fee.

When planning your nature excursions, it's always a good idea to visit the specific websites of the reserves or parks to obtain the latest information regarding admission fees, guided tours, and seasonal considerations. Embrace the natural wonders that the Harz region has to offer, where each protected area tells a unique story of ecological richness that is unparalleled.

Indulge in the tantalizing flavors of Harz's local cuisine, a culinary adventure that showcases the region's rich cultural heritage and bountiful natural resources. From hearty mountain dishes to delectable sweets, immerse yourself in the diverse gastronomic offerings that make Harz a paradise for food enthusiasts.

1. Harzer Cheese:

Embark on your gastronomic journey with Harzer Käse, a unique sour milk cheese. This regional delicacy comes in various shapes and sizes, boasting a robust flavor that pairs perfectly with crusty bread and locally brewed beer.

2. Braunkohl mit Pinkel:

Embrace the comforting warmth of Braunkohl mit Pinkel, a traditional winter dish. This hearty meal features kale slow-cooked with bacon, accompanied by smoky Pinkel sausage. A staple during festive gatherings, it warms both body and soul.

3. Harzer Wurst:

Delight in the savory goodness of Harzer Wurst, a smoked sausage crafted from finely ground pork. Whether enjoyed as a quick snack or as part of an authentic Harz breakfast spread, this delectable treat shines when paired with freshly baked bread.

4. Forellenhof Wernigerode:

Embark on an epicurean voyage at Forellenhof Wernigerode, an esteemed restaurant renowned for its trout specialties. Nestled in a picturesque setting, this culinary haven offers a delightful menu featuring locally sourced trout prepared in various mouthwatering ways.

5. Harzer Stracke:

Awaken your taste buds with Harzer Stracke, a dry-cured and smoked sausage bursting with flavor. Often savored sliced on bread or incorporated into charcuterie platters, this exquisite sausage pays homage to the region's time-honored meat craftsmanship.

6. Klöße:

Don't miss out on Klöße, the German rendition of dumplings that frequently graces the side of plates. These delectable potato or bread-based dumplings perfectly complement meat dishes and hold a cherished place in Harz's culinary repertoire.

7. Baumkuchen:

Conclude your epicurean adventure on a sweet note with Baumkuchen, a traditional layered cake resembling the rings of a tree. Revel in the moist and luscious layers, commonly found in local bakeries and pastry shops, leaving your taste buds enchanted.

8. Harzer Brot:

Discover the rustic charm of Harzer Brot, a dense and flavorsome rye bread. This traditional staple beautifully accompanies local cheeses, sausages, and spreads, adding an extra layer of authenticity to your culinary experience.

9. Kräuterlikör (Herb Liqueur):

Raise a toast with Harz's Kräuterlikör, an herbal liqueur celebrated for its aromatic blend of regional herbs. Whether enjoyed as an appetizing prelude or a satisfying digestif, this libation captures the essence of the majestic Harz Mountains through its unique flavors.

10. Coffee Culture in Wernigerode:

Immerse yourself in Wernigerode's vibrant coffee culture as you unwind in charming cafes exuding cozy ambiance. Indulge in freshly brewed coffee paired with delectable local pastries for an enchanting coffee experience that will leave you craving more.

As you savor the exquisite delicacies of Harz, you'll unearth a tapestry of flavors deeply intertwined with the region's cultural roots. Whether reveling in robust cheeses, savoring hearty stews, or succumbing to sweet temptations, Harz's culinary offerings promise an unforgettable journey for your palate

Prepare to be captivated by the stunning transformations that take place in the Harz region as it transitions through each season, revealing its unique charm and a vibrant array of colors that paint the landscape. From blossoming blooms to snow-covered peaks, here are the highlights of each season that you won't want to miss:

Spring: Blooms and Renewal (March to May)

As winter bids its farewell, nature awakens in a magnificent display of blossoming flora and revitalized landscapes.

- Nature's Awakening: Witness a magical transformation as meadows are carpeted with an array of flowers and trees burst into life.

- Explore Ilsetal Valley: Embark on enchanting hiking trails in Ilsetal Valley, where wildflowers accompany your every step, filling the air with their delightful fragrance.

- Discover Thale Hexentanzplatz: Capture breathtaking views adorned with blooming wildflowers at Thale Hexentanzplatz, adding a splash of color to an already mesmerizing panorama.

Summer: Outdoor Bliss and Festive Celebrations (June to August)
Summer unveils a playground of outdoor adventures and lively festivities, making it an ideal time for exploration.
- Adventure in Bode Gorge: Immerse yourself in nature's wonders as you engage in thrilling activities like hiking amidst lush greenery in Bode Gorge.
- Step Back in Time at Stolberg Festival: Transport yourself back to medieval times during Stolberg Festival, where lively events and historical reenactments bring history to life.
- Relax by Eckerstausee Reservoir: Indulge in water-based activities such as boating or enjoy leisurely lakeside picnics at Eckerstausee Reservoir.

Autumn: A Tapestry of Colors (September to November)
As autumn unfolds, the Harz region transforms into a breathtaking canvas painted with warm hues, offering a visual feast for the senses.
- Hike to Brocken Summit: Embark on an unforgettable hike to Brocken Summit, where you'll be rewarded with panoramic views of the Harz Mountains adorned in their stunning autumnal splendor.
- Quedlinburg Old Town Stroll: Take a leisurely stroll through Quedlinburg's Old Town, where cobblestone streets come alive with a vibrant tapestry of fall colors.

- Scenic Train Ride on Harz Narrow Gauge Railways: Immerse yourself in the golden foliage of autumn as you embark on a scenic train ride through the majestic mountains.

Winter: Frosty Delights and Snowy Adventures (December to February)

Winter blankets the Harz region in a serene layer of snow, inviting you to embrace the enchantment of this magical season.

- Capture Wernigerode Castle's Fairytale Charm: Marvel at the fairytale ambiance of Wernigerode Castle as it becomes adorned with glistening snow against a picturesque winter backdrop.

- Explore Brocken Trails on Snowshoes: Embark on an exhilarating adventure through the snowy trails of Brocken, discovering a winter wonderland at its highest peak.
- Immerse Yourself in Christmas Markets: Experience the festive spirit at Christmas markets in charming towns like Quedlinburg and Wernigerode. Lose yourself amidst twinkling lights and indulge in seasonal delights.

Whether you find yourself captivated by spring's bloom, summer's warmth, autumn's vibrant colors or winter's enchantment, each month in the Harz region unveils its own unique treasures. Plan your visit accordingly and prepare to witness the ever-changing allure of this picturesque destination.